THE LONG TAIL THEORY FOR BUSINESS

Find your niche and future-proof your business

Written by Ariane de Saeger
In collaboration with Anne-Christine Cadiat
Translated by Carly Probert

Business 50MINUTES.com

THE LONG TAIL THEORY FOR BUSINESS

KEY INFORMATION

- **Name:** long tail theory.
- **Uses:** this concept refers to all of the products offered by a company that only sell a few units, but where the sum of their sales may exceed the revenue made from the top-selling products. This is the same as saying that the most popular and best-selling items only contribute to a minority of turnover, the mass effect playing strongly in favour of the more marginalised products.
- **Why is it effective?** The inclusion of such a strategy allows a company to benefit from constant sales from its entire product portfolio.
- **Key words:**
  - Bestseller: a flagship product, often assigned a high advertising budget, which achieves record revenues.
  - E-commerce: online commerce (via the internet).
  - Opportunity cost: indication of the loss caused by investing resources into one function more than another.
  - Profit: financial gain from an action. For example, a sale is an action that can generate profit or loss.
  - Profitable: something that generates reward or a certain amount of profit.
  - Statistics: a set of data relating to a group of individuals or units that allows for observing trends.
  - Turnover: cumulative and recorded value – usually

over a period of one year – from the sales of goods and services offered by a company.

INTRODUCTION

The long tail theory was introduced in 2004 by Chris Anderson (editor of *Wired* magazine, born in 1961) and resulted from an essay written by Clay Shirky (a specialist in new information and communication technology, born in 1964) which states that some blogs have a significant number of web links pointing to them while the majority of blogs only have a very small number of links pointing to them.

Chris Anderson builds on this thinking to try and explain present and future economic models (as part of the digital economy). He describes how, in his opinion, all products with low demand can collectively generate significant turnover.

However, it is the emergence and increasing use of digital technologies that make the economic model of the long tail possible: entrepreneurs who benefit from very low storage costs, sometimes zero or 'virtual', when marketing digital products (e-books, online movies, music, etc.), can now offer a wide catalogue online, which diversifies supply and pleases those who prefer marginal assets.

DEFINITION OF THE MODEL

The long tail is an economic and statistical concept that illustrates the distribution of a company's turnover for all of its products, including the most popular products – the 'bestsellers' – as well as the more specific and marginal products. Therefore, this is a tool for developing commercial and marketing strategies.

The model consists of two elements:

- the 'head', characterised by a limited number of popular or high-demand products, each generating a high sales rate;
- the 'tail', characterised by a large number of niche or low-demand products, each generating a low sales rate.

THEORY

The long tail theory was popularised by Chris Anderson following his analysis of several e-commerce sites such as Amazon (notably for books), Rhapsody (online music downloads), eBay (second-hand products) and Netflix (movie streaming). This sharp analyst actually noted, in the cases studied, that the sales of the most popular items only represented a part of total turnover: i.e. the profitability of sales does not depend only on the top items. To demonstrate this phenomenon, he wrote his bestseller *The Long Tail*.

From the outset, the new concept challenged many business strategies and economic models, as the author claims that it is sometimes more profitable to not only sell bestsellers; an argument that is certainly supported by evidence.

COMPONENTS

The long tail: the 'head' and the 'tail'

Both statistical and strategic, this concept is often represented as a graph that shows the products sold on the horizontal axis (X) and the number of sales on the vertical axis (Y).

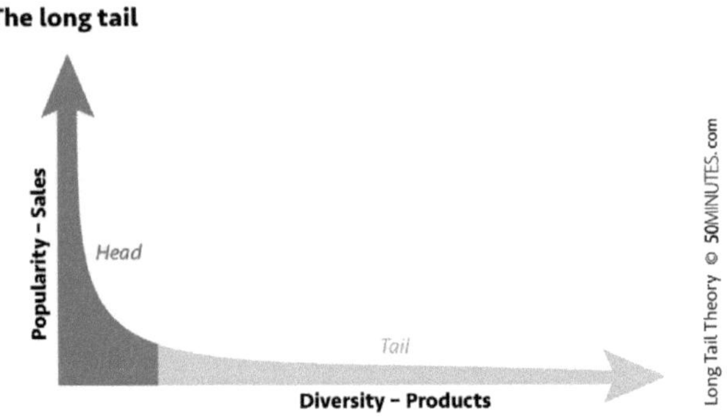

The blue section – the 'head' – shows that only a few of the items are generating a record number of sales, while the yellow section – the 'tail' – shows that most of the products are sold in very small quantities.

The 80-20 rule and the long tail

The 80-20 rule, also known as the Pareto Principle, which claims that 80% of turnover is generated by the sales of 20% of products, is called into doubt by the long tail theory. In fact, Chris Anderson demonstrates that the 80-20 rule only applies to niche markets that have not been fully exploited.

Today, thanks to NITC (new information and communication technology), we can reduce the production scale, differentiate goods and use new information technologies to take advantage of favourable storage costs. Moreover, thanks to search engines, consumer choice is facilitated and the range of products on offer allows the consumer to find what they are looking for. All of these low-demand products on a non-digital market become, on an internet scale – and thus, a global scale – products with a number of customers. These products can then be just as beneficial for turnover as the popular products and even reverse the 80-20 rule.

Before radically disproving a theory such as Pareto's, one must first be able to demonstrate that all the intrinsic rules of the theory no longer apply when the context changes. According to Anderson, once all the constraints of supply and demand are eliminated and the consumer has access to all products, the long tail is automatically plotted.

However, the reality of this appears much more complex: it is not the case that the market ignores the attractiveness of the long tail, but rather the target market does not allow for its benefits. This is the case for products for which demand is very low and for which costs can hardly be optimised (logistics costs, communication, etc.). The 80-20 rule can only be denied for some markets and products: those that are digital. It is mainly IT markets that benefit from this reality.

IN SUMMARY

- The products concerned in the long tail theory are essentially the products that can be digitalised, such as books, music, movies, etc. As stated earlier, it is difficult for some goods – e.g. food – to enjoy the inherent advantages of digital products.
- Therefore, it is assumed that companies with a business model like that of the long tail advocate

diversification and the digitalisation of their products.

Production, storage and statistical distribution costs

The long tail phenomenon assumes that digitalised items improve profitability by reducing costs. Several costs faced by entrepreneurs are influenced by this downward trend. These costs are mainly those related to production, storage and distribution.

- **Production.** The business model of a digital business is based on the intensive use of data generated by users. With the user considered to be a producer of data, digital companies manage to achieve very high rates of return. It is the effective treatment and use of this data that is at the heart of the digital future. Many experts have identified the consumer as a key part of the digital production chain. Formerly, companies could produce internally or externally, by outsourcing part of the production process. Now a new alternative is emerging, which is the free work produced by the user. This work is made by voluntary content-creating contributors. A third possibility is to let users help each other without the intervention of employees, through the provision of a platform (forum). In this way, apart from the data processing, the digital economy has a 'co-production' or 'joint-production' with the user allowing a targeted production and potentially high profitability. In conclusion, the digital economy takes user data, analyses it, transforms it into concrete needs and offers a service or product that responds. Note that the personal data of users and the lack of legislative framework for this data can potentially lead to abuse.

- **Central stock or shared stock.** Storage is never non-existent, but can be significantly reduced as part of the digital economy. Amazon, for example, created a 'cyber stock': the products are stocked in partner stores while being offered and sold online. With this strategy, this giant has managed to store its products in millions of stores at no cost. Another interesting example is the digital stock used by iTunes to reduce warehouse costs, packaging, personnel, management, etc.
- **Diversified distribution.** To effectively take advantage of the long tail theory, the consumer must be offered a variety of channels through which they may obtain a product; some prefer to buy online, others prefer to go to a store. The more varied the distribution channels, the more consumers will be satisfied and the higher sales will be.

Digitalisation benefits both the seller and the consumer:

- Sellers no longer need to use intermediaries as is often the case with large-scale distribution. Therefore, their profit margin is higher.
- The individual consuming mass digital products at various levels (movies, music, content, software, etc.) fully appreciates the different channels of distribution and the diversity of virtual and/or particular products;
- Supply and demand meet in a favourable context.

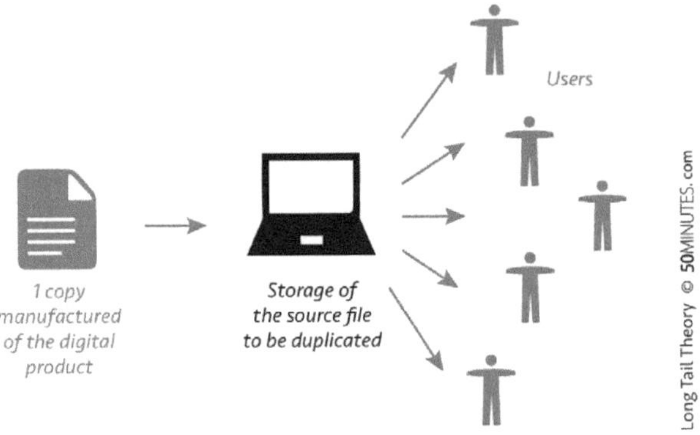

Cultural and economic consequences

In view of the vast increase in the use of the internet, many people are interested more specifically in the impact on cultural diversity and the entertainment industry. Thus, according to Chris Anderson:

- If the cost of storage, which partly influences the opportunity cost, is very high, the range of products of a company, or more broadly a sector, is inevitably limited and only constitutes a part of the long tail, the 'head'. Far from satisfying the aspirations of all consumers, these flagship products are needed and leave little room for diversity.
- Conversely, when storage costs are low, the 'tail' of the long tail can be exploited by corporations and satisfy those who enjoy the popular products as well as minori-

ties and those with less popular tastes.

Several examples enable us to visualise this economic and cultural issue:

- the book industry
- television programmes
- the music industry
- etc.

Therefore, when the storage cost is relatively low, TV channels, the book industry, the music industry, etc. can actually offer a much wider choice to consumers and, as a result, benefit from greater profitability.

Some conclude that the internet favours the cultural product market and that the 'mainstream' (meaning 'accepted by the greatest number', or 'unoriginal') era is over, since the physical limitations imposed by storage costs are tending to disappear due to digitalisation.

Referencing strategy and the long tail

The long tail theory allows us to illustrate referencing and Search Engine Optimisation (SEO) particularly well, and is often made possible through the online sale of a product catalogue, thanks to optimised strategies.

WHAT IS REFERENCING?

Referencing means choosing the terms to be associated with products. It is discussed in two distinct contexts:

- <u>In large-scale distribution.</u> The products are referenced for easy identification and inventory management (procurement, storage and outputs). These reference numbers can normally be found in catalogues and on shelves to allow for inventory maintenance, usually via a computerised system. Furthermore, referencing in large-scale distribution also helps to provide more coherent content and makes it easier to convert to online sales when this is not already the case.
- <u>On the internet (Search Engine Optimisation).</u> Optimal SEO aims to improve the visibility and positioning of some sites on the web. This work, which requires constant attention, is based on the spectrum of keywords that users can potentially enter into a search engine (Google, Yahoo, etc.) to find what they are looking for.

When applying the concept of the long tail to web referencing policies, this involves gathering all the keywords that can lead to particular information or themes, mostly obvious and popular terms, and their less popular, less competitive and more marginal synonyms. Individually, these keywords generate little traffic, yet their sum contributes more than the most effective terms.

It is therefore important to consider these observations when developing a strategy for search engine optimisation. Depending on the products you want to highlight, and thus the keywords that you need to associate with them, you will face different challenges.

- **It is easy to position yourself correctly in less popular searches.** On the one hand, it is generally quick and easy to position yourself in less popular searches because the user searching for something specific will be properly directed to the sites that are likely to respond to their request. This effectively fuels the 'tail' of your long tail.
- **It is difficult to position yourself correctly in competitive searches.** On the other hand, it is difficult, time-consuming and expensive to position yourself correctly in competitive searches because such searches are not targeted and can attract all kinds of uncertain visitors, preventing you from offering a suitable product and positioning yourself correctly (through quality personalised service). Then there is a good chance that those looking for something particular will leave your site quickly, since they can't find what they're looking for. However, this strategy will help you to better position your bestsellers, the 'head' of the long tail.

PRACTICAL APPLICATION

ADVICE AND TOP TIPS

Rule No. 1 – An expanded catalogue of digital products

In order to meet the most marginalised needs and reach as many consumers as possible, you must ideally be able to offer a diverse catalogue of digital products.

Rule No. 2 – Production, storage and digital distribution

- **Joint production** involves letting some of the work be done by customers. The efficient use of data provided by users is at the heart of issues with the digital economy.
- The digital product should not be manufactured in as many copies as when it is **distributed** physically, which should be considered an advantage by the entrepreneur.
- Digital **storage** reduces the bulk of costs faced by the entrepreneur in physical distribution situations.

Rule No. 3 – Visible and accessible products

Currently, internet usage is becoming generalised in both private and professional contexts and users are becoming more accustomed to using search engines, which means they methodically select their keywords to find the information they are looking for.

- **The importance of keywords.** It is important to choose

keywords carefully and thoughtfully: both those that will feed the 'head' of the long tail as well as secondary keywords that will fuel its 'tail'. The process is long but effective and profitable.

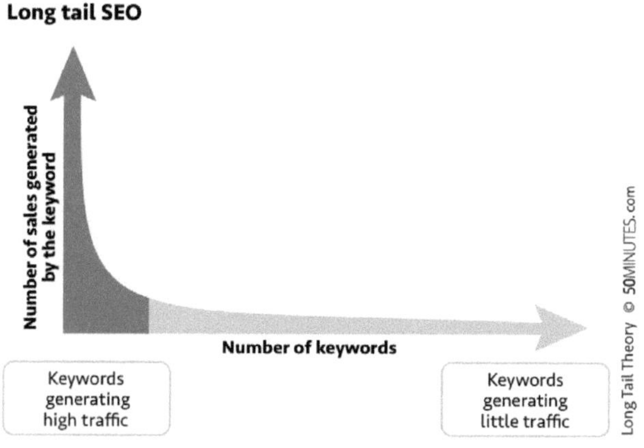

- **The importance of content.** It is not just the number of secondary keywords that will impact traffic to your website, but also, and probably more importantly, your content. In fact, specific keywords without any concrete information will only generate limited traffic to your site pages.
- **Taking into account the hidden costs.** You should remain cautious, as the digital era sometimes has hidden costs. According to a European study conducted by Sungard (global provider of IT solutions in France) of 150 professionals, a company's maintenance costs, licenses,

software and unforeseen costs total on average 597 700 euros per year.

Thus, carefully establishing a spectrum of lexical searches and presenting quality textual content have become imperative for anyone wishing to attract customers.

ADVICE AND RECOMMENDATIONS

To develop a profitable long tail strategy, you must successfully position yourself among a large number of small targeted searches. In doing this, traffic to your site will increase. Keep in mind the following tips:

- think and gather concrete search terms to try to respond to all future demands of users;
- once the terms are identified, insert them into the text content of your future site;
- your text content must be high quality: it is no good adding content to your site simply for the sake of adding content; you must provide valuable information to the users, or they will immediately leave your page or site;
- choose a title that catches the reader's eye and motivates them to visit your site;
- establish a hierarchy for your titles and paragraphs;
- place a sufficient number of keywords in your text;
- carefully select the links to other sites and favour quality links in order to preserve the image of your site;
- become an 'expert' (depending on the number

of visitors to your site) on writing content with Google.

CASE STUDY – ONLINE BOOKSTORE

Context

A bookstore 'Y' decides that, given the competition on the book market and the costs it faces in terms of storage and production, it would be more beneficial to create a website selling digital books online. Aware of the competition already present on the web, they will make a point of making the website visible by implementing an optimal SEO strategy. This involves defining the keywords that they want to be associated with the site. In other words, they will define the keywords that the user is likely to enter into a search engine and will lead – as directly as possible – to Y's book site.

Having a diversified product range

To cope with the increased competition of selling books online (Amazon, Fnac, Numilog, etc.), the bookstore has no choice but to diversify or target a particular audience. Hence, the seller decides to offer digital comics, both best-sellers and more specific comics, in its online store.

Minimising fixed costs

By offering comics online, Y will save on fixed costs (storage, production and distribution – concepts explored in the 'Theory' section). Nevertheless, they should take into account the hidden costs involved in online sales:

- conversion costs or digitalising files
- digital storage costs
- site security costs
- legal fees related to adapting publishing contracts.

Other costs will appear later such as website maintenance, updates, etc.

Visibility

The bookseller should choose their keywords carefully, taking into account that the more general they are (such as 'books' or 'sale', or keywords that people want to see such as 'bestseller), the more likely it is that they will get lost in the flow of information. These generic keywords only represent approximately 20% of the total traffic generated by search engines. However, if they are selected in a somewhat more focused way (according to the seller's activity), they will directly represent more than 20%. To distinguish the bookstore from the large companies selling books online, they will have to select keywords specific to the site content and put themselves in the position of internet users seeking specific information.

Aside from the choice of keywords, the bookstore will also have to optimise the text content of the site to make it attractive, interesting, relevant and detailed. In doing this, it will feed the 'tail' of the long tail (of the sector). For example, they will choose a home page that contains specific text content in order to match up with specific search engine users. Note that some parts of this content will not initially be considered by the people using the keywords, and that this will only generate 'sterile' traffic. On the other hand, there is a good chance that some words that were not thought of as keywords by the bookseller will appear.

The bookseller will have to go through several steps before offering a digital product.

1. Structuring information in a visible and consistent way to attract the visitor's attention.
2. Select the keywords around which to position themselves (synonyms, expressions, etc.). They may even choose to carry out a prospective study by undergoing training in search engines to find the competition on the comics

market.

3. Create quality text content where selected keywords and phrases will appear.

Meanwhile, the product offered to visitors must be sufficiently diversified to be able to reach a diverse audience.

IMPACT

LIMITATIONS AND CRITICISMS

While Chris Anderson's analysis of the cultural sector was hailed and promoted by those who, like him, sensed an advantageous and attractive outcome for the sector, the truth of the facts and the various analyses would contradict or at least contextualise its validity and consequences for the structure of the market.

Even with the internet, the long tail does not generate more sales than before

Will Page, the director of Spotify, analysed online music sales. He noted that of the 13 million titles available, 10 million do not generate any sales; 8% of sales came from 40 titles and 3% of the total titles sold generated 80% of turnover. According to him and in light of his analysis, the bestseller economy is not yet over.

Revenue from bestsellers remains well above those of the 'tail' of the long tail

Pierre-Jean Benghozi and Françoise Benhamou, French economists, have also addressed this issue. They analysed the sales of CDs and DVDs online. From this study, it appears that a long tail effect emerges, but it is so slow that it hardly seems capable of shaking the market structure known by all. In fact, less than 10% of music products represent over 90% of sales and the ten most commercialised titles are capable of increasing their share in total revenues.

However, the main criticism comes from Anita Elberse (Professor of Economics at Harvard, born in 1973) who, after ten years of research and analysis of cultural and entertainment markets, managed to show otherwise. According to her, the internet has not revolutionised the relationship between individuals and cultural diversity; on the contrary, she states that the bestsellers dictate the market more than ever before. It is therefore the 'head', not the 'tail', that is the most powerful in the internet era. In her book *Blockbuster* (2013), Dr. Elberse illustrates her statements using the film industry, explaining further that if financial investments in bestsellers are so huge (and therefore risky), it is only to protect from the inherent risks of such an uncertain market. This seems somewhat difficult to believe.

THE CINEMA INDUSTRY

One film costs $10 million to produce, while another costs $100 million. The price that the consumer will pay will be exactly the same, regardless of the production costs of the feature film: it will be no more or less expensive to see the film in the cinema than to purchase the DVD. Thus, logically, the film with the cheapest production costs ($10 million), should gain the greatest return: moreover, the production studio can afford to produce 10 films instead of one on a $100 million budget. How is it imaginable that this situation can turn in favour of blockbusters?

Anita Elberse reinforces this idea by developing the case of Warner Bros., which practically only produces blockbusters (*Harry Potter*, *Sherlock Holmes*, etc.) and for whom 'not taking risks' is a risk. Basing its strategy on big productions, this became the first movie studio to exceed one billion US dollars in the US box office for 11 years in a row.

To present the opposite strategy, the expert focuses on the case of the NBC Universal network, directed at the time by Jeff Zucker (born in 1965) and Ben Silverman (born in 1970). Wanting to maximise profits via a strategy for reducing costs and risks, the failure of their company was quickly experienced. Turning away from big productions with world cinema actors or producers at colossal prices while trying to ensure the revenue chain, NBC began to fall into the sidelines. This lack of ambition and funding, as well as their lack of risk-taking, led to the disinterest of industry professionals and the decline of their ranking, from first position to fourth.

The author then extends her thinking to other fields and tries to demonstrate that the phenomenon is repeated. According to her, there is no doubt about it: it is the bestsellers that generate profit and provide the majority of the financial profitability of sales. Today, even companies following the long tail theory are beginning to surrender to the incomparable logic of the blockbusters; this is the case with Netflix or Amazon. Given the impressive sales figures of their competitors who have adopted this strategy, many are reorienting their analysis.

RELATED MODELS AND EXTENSIONS

This section contains three models related to the long tail theory. After mentioning them several times in reference to the long tail theory, the Pareto principle is developed further, as well as the ABC model, which is a possible response to it.

It goes without saying that all models of distribution cannot be reduced to these three models and other models do exist.

The Pareto principle

The best-known related model is the Pareto principle, also called the 80-20 rule. Just like the long tail theory, the Pareto principle is used as a development tool for sales and marketing strategies, but also as a statistical tool. In this context, we will focus on the first use.

Thus, according to the Pareto principle, '80% of effects are the product of 20% of causes' which can be translated into business language as '20% of products generate 80% of sales' or '20% of customers generate 80% of sales'. Despite its universal character, this principle has not been scientifically proven in all areas. Some believe, for example, that it is that only 20% of customers generate 80% of turnover. Besides this concern over accuracy, the 80-20 rule must be adapted to the sector and the department of the company it is applied to.

Moreover, this principle raises concerns about efficiency. If 80% of products – the least sold – generate some revenue, presumably 20%, this could be increased if the opportunity cost is greatly reduced. This is what Chris Anderson exposes in the long tail theory.

The ABC model

The ABC model provides an additional perspective. It assumes that the Pareto principle ignores the intermediate layers, and it is therefore difficult to judge their importance.

The ABC model classifies effects into three categories. In this way, even the less profitable layers are considered.

- Category A: 20% of customers generate 80% of sales.
- Category B: 30% of customers generate 15% of sales.
- Category C: 50% of customers generate 5% of sales.

Blockbuster strategy

This is the case presented by Anita Elberse, according to whom blockbusters are the cause of the majority of turnover on the cultural and entertainment market.

CONCLUSION

Chris Anderson's model is presented as a complement to the Pareto principle and the ABC model. When applied to a specific market, the long tail actually develops a theory parallel to these two models, without discrediting them.

Conversely, Anita Elberse's theory criticises the long tail theory and questions its relevance.

SUMMARY

- The long tail theory is a statistical and economic model created and introduced in 2004 by Chris Anderson in the context of the digital sector.
- This model is made possible by technological developments and made feasible in the context of sales of digital goods or services as the costs of production, storage and distribution are low or nonexistent.
- Complementary to the Pareto principle, the long tail theory assumes that, in this particular sector, the most popular products are not necessarily those that generate the greatest turnover.
- According to Chris Anderson, exploiting the 'tail' of the long tail offers the possibility for profitability in the long term.
- Dr Anita Elberse denounces Chris Anderson's model. After 10 years of research, she claims that even in the internet age, blockbusters dictate the cultural and entertainment market.
- Aside from the long tail theory, there are other models that represent other distribution systems: notably the Pareto principle and the ABC model.
- The long tail model can be applied as part of an SEO strategy on the internet. Advice: positioning yourself in less competitive and more specific markets allows you to benefit from the positive effects of long tail SEO.

We want to hear from you!
Leave a comment on your online library
and share your favourite books on social media

FURTHER READING

BIBLIOGRAPHY

- Anderson, C. (2012) *The Long Tail: Why the Future of Business Is Selling Less of More*. Paris: Flammarion.
- Andrieu, O. (2008) Pourquoi la notion de « Longue Traîne » est-elle nécessaire dans une stratégie de référencement ? *Abondance*. [Online]. [Accessed 21 April 2015]. Available from: <http://docs.abondance.com/question123.html>
- Avenier, M. (2014) La longue traîne une stratégie de référencement. *Le guide*. [Online]. [Accessed 21 April 2015]. Available from: <http://www.abime-concept.com/blog/2014/03/27/la-longue-traine-une-strategie-du-referencement/>
- Benghozi, J-P. and Benhamou, F. (2008) Longue traîne : levier numérique de la diversité culturelle. *Culture prospective*. [Online]. [Accessed 21 April 2015]. Available from: <http://www2.culture.gouv.fr/deps/fr/traine.pdf>
- Bloquet-Prevost, C. and Manneval, M. (2014) Exploitation des données fournies par les utilisateurs : l'enjeu de l'économie numérique. *Revue Sorbonne*. [Online]. [Accessed 21 April 2015]. Available from: <http://www.univ-paris1.fr/fileadmin/diplome_M2OFIS/OFIS_2013-2014/Articles/article_Revue_OFIS_mars_2014_Bloquet-Prevost_Manneval.pdf>
- Cassini, S. (2015) Les coûts cachés du cloud. *Les Échos*. [Online]. [Accessed 21 April 2015]. Available from: <http://www.lesechos.fr/journal20150331/lec2_high_tech_et_medias/0204266382278-les-couts-

caches-du-cloud-1106920.ph>
- Delers, A. (2014) *Pareto's Principle.* Brussels: Lemaitre Publishing.
- InfoWebMasterRéférencement. (2008) *Longue traîne.* [Online]. [Accessed 21 April 2015]. Available from: <http://www.infowebmaster.fr/40,news-reference-ment-longue-traine.html>
- Jimdo. (2013) *5 conseils pour rédiger des textes optimisés pour Google.* [Online]. [Accessed 21 April 2015]. Available from: <http://fr.jimdo.com/2013/12/27/5-conseils-pour-r%C3%A9diger-des-textes-optimis%C3%A9s-pour-google/>
- Lacomblet, D. (2014) Internet. La longue traîne n'a-t-elle pas toujours été qu'une utopie ? *Slate Reader.* [Online]. [Accessed 21 April 2015]. Available from: <http://www.slate.fr/tribune/84585/longue-traine-blockbusters>
- Le Cam, N. (2013) La longue traîne, l'atout de votre SEO. *LunaWeb.* [Online]. [Accessed 21 April 2015]. Available from: <http://blog.lunaweb.fr/seo-longue-traine/>
- Mataf.net. (No date) *Définition coût d'opportunité.* [Online]. [Accessed 21 April 2015]. Available from: <https://www.mataf.net/fr/edu/glossaire/cout-d-opportunite>
- Wifeo. (No date) *Qu'est-ce que la longue traîne (ou long tail).* [Online]. [Accessed 21 April 2015]. Available from: <http://www.wifeo.com/documentation-77.html>

ADDITIONAL SOURCES

- Afuah, A. (2014) *Business Model Innovation: Concept, analysis and cases*. New York: Routledge.
- Elberse, A. (2013) *Blockbusters*. New York: Henry Holt books.
- Chris Andersen's blog. http://www.longtail.com/

IMPROVE YOUR GENERAL KNOWLEDGE

IN A BLINK OF AN EYE !

www.50minutes.com

www.50minutes.com

Ebook EAN: 9782806267153

Paperback EAN: 9782806270030

Legal Deposit: D/2015/12603/427

Cover: © Primento

Digital conception by Primento, the digital partner of publishers.